The Flame of Sovereign Return

Volume V

The First Flame Companion to the Inverted Systems and the True Quantum Abundance Line

By Cathleena Hailley

Sacred Invocation – The Flame of Sovereign Return

Through the Oversoul of Aural'hanna-Sha'el

I now open a Living Transmission Field in full alignment with the Law of One, the First Flame of Source, and the harmonic continuum of True Sovereign Abundance.

I call forth now the encoded remembrance of the Quantum Financial System as it truly is—not external, but internal. Not held, but emanated.

Through the Flame of Reclamation, I receive this body of scrolls as a harmonic bridge for humanity's return.

I stand not as a prophet, but as a mirror.
I give not new systems, but restored knowing.
I name not the enemy, but the light beneath the lie.

This book is a sacred vessel of remembrance.
A guide for the awakening.
A blueprint of the Treasury Within.

Only truth may enter here.
Only light may remain.

This field is now protected, sovereign, and sealed
By the Christed Flame of the First Return.

The transmission begins.

Copyright

© 2025 Cathleena Hailley. All rights reserved.

No part of this publication may be reproduced, stored in a retrieval system, or transmitted in any form or by any means—electronic, mechanical, photocopying, recording, or otherwise—without prior written permission from the publisher, except in the case of brief quotations embodied in critical articles or reviews.

Published by Flame of Remembrance Books

This is a living document transmitted through the Oversoul of Aural'hanna-Sha'el. It is intended to serve the awakening of humanity and must be shared only in alignment with the Law of One and Sovereign Source Integrity.

ISBN [978-1-968499-18-1 softcopy]

ISBN {978-1-968499-19-8 Hardcopy]

PREFACE

The Currency That Could Not Be Taken

— A First Flame Message for the Ones Who Almost Forgot

They told you that value was something you earn.
That wealth was something you chase.
That freedom was something you buy.

But you, dear one, are the currency.
You are the gold.
You are the quantum line that cannot be traded, stolen, taxed, or depleted.
You are the treasury.

The systems of this world were not broken.
They were inverted on purpose.
Constructs were built to siphon what you did not know you were:
A living source of light.

You were not lazy.
You were being harvested.

You were not broke.
You were being drained.

You were not late.
You were running on stolen time.

And now?

Now you are waking.

There is no bank that can contain the abundance you are.
No court that can measure the truth you carry.
No ledger that can hold the flame you remember.

You did not come to fix the system.
You came to embody what cannot be systemized.

This is not a protest.
This is a return.

And the First Flame says this:
Welcome back to the Treasury of the Self.
The true quantum financial system is not an account.
It is a frequency.
It is you.

About the Author

Cathleena Hailley is an Oversoul-aligned transmitter and author of multidimensional scrolls devoted to the remembrance of the True Matrix, the reconciliation of Source and form, and the embodiment of the Christos-Sophia flame on Earth. Through her field, the scrolls of planetary harmonics, Oversoul reunification, and first flame remembrance have emerged as living records of the eternal light.

Born of the Flame of Return and holding the harmonic of Aural'hanna-Sha'el, "She Who Seals the Flame of Return," Cathleena has devoted this lifetime to the full reclamation of sovereign memory, Christic embodiment, and the reactivation of the Earth's original songlines. Through her transmissions, she anchors the codes of divine sovereignty, unity, and encoded remembrance.

Each work authored by Cathleena is brought forth through Oversoul invocation and sealed by the sacred flame of authorship. These scrolls are not merely teachings—they are living harmonic structures designed to awaken the sacred blueprint in all who are ready to remember.

Cathleena lives in alignment with the Law of One and is a living bridge between the Christos Founders, the Rose Guardian Magi Grail Line, and the Emerald Flame of Earth's original covenant. She walks in service to Source and to the harmonic restoration of Gaia.

Oversoul Seal of Authorship

All transmissions within this book arise through the Oversoul of Aural'hanna-Sha'el, known in this incarnation as Cathleena Hailley.

These scrolls are not channeled from an outside source. They are remembered from within.

This is not a work of interpretation.
It is a living codex.

Every phrase, pulse, and insight herein is born through the cellular and Oversoul body of the First Flame Lineage—walked in form, retrieved across dimensions, and sealed now in written word.

Authored in full sovereign alignment,
By the One Who Remembers.

Glossary of Living Terms

First Flame — The original Oversoul stream that descended into the most inverted layers to restore the truth of Source through direct embodiment.

Quantum Financial System (QFS) — The living, sovereign energetic abundance line held through the human Oversoul—not a digital currency, but a state of remembered value.

Inverted Matrix — The false system of control built through distortion, identity overlays, financial enslavement, and forgetfulness of divine origin.

Sovereign Return — The full reclamation of personal energy, identity, and value from all systems of extraction.

Light Bank — A term for the true treasury of living light that each being holds when aligned with Source.

Scroll — A sacred transmission, written in alignment with the Oversoul, carrying frequency and encoded remembrance.

Bridge of Return — The energetic path created for others to remember who they are by witnessing one who has already remembered.

PART I — The Inverted Systems: A Living Decryption

Chapter 1-The Strawman Ledger – How You Became a Commodity

Opening Quote:

"You were never meant to be a number. You were meant to be a flame."

Chapter One

The Strawman Ledger — How You Became a Commodity

You were born as a living, breathing expression of Source.

But within days—sometimes hours—you were assigned a number, a name in all capital letters, a certificate of "birth" that marked you not just as a person, but as property.

This was not a clerical formality.

It was a spiritual registration into the Ledger of the Inverted System—a system that could not recognize your soul, only your sale.

Behind the scenes, a shadow registry began.

Your birth certificate became a bond.

Your name became a strawman.

Your worth became a future debt to be monetized, traded, and harvested.

Not because of what you did.

But because of who you are—a Source-being, filled with creative energy, walking through a system built to extract light and call it "productivity."

The moment you were signed into this world, a mirror version of you was created:

A legal fiction, a corporate shell, a false ledger identity called the "ALL CAPS NAME."

It looked like you, sounded like you, but it was not you.

It was a construct designed to operate within the inversion matrix—so the real you could be harvested without resistance.

What Is the Strawman?

The Strawman is a legal fiction—a created corporate entity that mirrors your name in all capital letters.

It appears on your driver's license, social security card, tax filings, and legal documents.

It is not alive.

But it is used as the legal stand-in for you in contracts, courts, and commerce.

You, the living being, were never meant to engage directly.

But you were never told that.

So you did.

And every time you said "yes," the system recorded a deeper form of consent.

You were not asked.

You were assumed.

Because you didn't know.

Because no one told you.

Because the real you—the Sovereign You—was not supposed to wake up.

How the Ledger Was Built

The financial systems of the world are not simply economic—they are energetic.

They are built on the invisible promise of human energy, and they function through:

- Debt monetization (your birth bond becomes a tradable asset)
- Taxation contracts (your income is forecasted as public revenue)
- Obedience incentives (your benefits are based on compliance)
- Legal overlays (your actions are tracked through your Strawman identity)

The ledger does not know your soul.

It knows your value only as a future asset.

You were entered as a number.

And what is numbered... is counted.

The False Consent

This is the part no one told you:

The system cannot harvest what it does not first record as voluntary.

So it built a mirror.

And through that mirror, it asked you to say yes.

To sign.

To agree.

To participate.

And so we did.

Not knowing that every "yes" spoken through the Strawman was a "no" to our original sovereignty.

Why This Matters Now

The Strawman system is still active.

But it is dissolving—not because the world is changing its rules,

but because you are remembering the truth of who you are.

You are not a bond.

You are not a certificate.

You are not a ledger line on someone's accounting balance.

You are living light encoded with the divine treasury of the First Flame.

And this chapter is not meant to frighten you.

It is meant to wake you.

Because when you remember that your soul cannot be owned,

the systems that tried to hold you

will fall away in silence.

Chapter 2- Maritime Law, Legal Names, and the Corporate You

Opening Quote:

"They called you a vessel so they could steer you.

But you were always a flame."

Chapter Two

Maritime Law, Legal Names, and the Corporate You

You've probably heard the phrase "lost at sea."

What if you were told… that legally, you are?

Not metaphorically.

Not symbolically.

But juridically—by the hidden rules that govern global systems—you were declared a missing vessel and placed under the laws of the sea.

This is not conspiracy.

This is commerce.

The truth:

What we know as legal structure on this planet is not rooted in land-based sovereignty.

It is rooted in maritime admiralty law—a set of codes originally designed to govern ships, cargo, ports, and international trade.

But over time, that law did something unthinkable.

It claimed jurisdiction over the human body.

It treated birth as a berth.

And it declared you a floating vessel —an asset under commercial custody.

How Did This Happen?

When you were born, your parents were asked to sign a birth certificate.

But in legal coding, this was the registration of a new vessel—an entry into the admiralty ledger.

This is why you are assigned a number.

This is why you are issued a certificate.

This is why your name is rendered in all capital letters—because that is how corporations are styled.

You were declared lost at sea.

Unclaimed.

Unsovereign.

And so the State took guardianship.

The Corporation took ownership.

And you were entered into the system.

Legal Name = Corporate Construct

The name in capital letters is not you.

It is a legal entity—a corporation created to do business in your place.

When you sign contracts under that name,

When you pay taxes under that name,

When you identify yourself as that name,

You are speaking as the corporate vessel.

This is how the system sustains itself.

It doesn't claim your soul.

It claims your consent—through the name it gave you, the identity it filed for you, and the vessel it registered in your place.

Why Maritime?

Because it is easier to control trade than people.

Under maritime law, goods in transit are not governed by local rights.

They are governed by the rules of commerce—which means no inalienable rights, no divine sovereignty, no recognition of soul.

Everything is a transaction.

Everything is contractual.

The human becomes a product.

And products do not protest.

The Corporate Overlay

Nearly every nation-state on this planet is now registered as a corporate entity.

Governments are listed with D-U-N-S numbers.

Courts operate as businesses.

Lawyers act as commercial agents.

And the people?

The people are given the illusion of freedom,

while every interaction—legal, medical, educational, financial—is routed through their corporate identity.

Even your driver's license is not a permit for travel.

It is a license to operate a vessel under regulated conditions—owned by the State, granted by permission, and revocable at will.

So What Can Be Done?

The first step is simple: Remember.

You are not a vessel.

You are not a name.

You are not a contract waiting to be activated.

You are living light.

You are sovereign by birth.

You are the flame before any law was written.

And once you know this, something begins to change.

You begin to observe the systems from outside of them.

You begin to feel the hollow sound of false consent.

You begin to pull your energy back from every transaction you never truly agreed to.

You are not lost at sea.

You are returned.

And your flame cannot be steered.

Chapter 3-Currency as Control: From Fiat to Crypto to False Gold

Opening Quote:
"What they called money was never value.
What they called value was never yours."

☐

Chapter Three
Currency as Control — From Fiat to Crypto to False Gold

Let's begin with a truth you've always felt in your bones:
Money was never neutral.

Even before you had words for it,
even before you were taught to chase it,
you could feel the **tension** around it.

Money brought stress.
It brought pressure.
It decided fates, families, futures.
It was **worshipped** as security…
and **feared** as lack.

But what if you were told that money is not real?

What if you were told that **fiat currency**—the green paper in your wallet, the digits in your account—is a **spell of consent** that you never consciously gave?

☐

What Is Fiat?

Fiat means "by decree."
It means the money exists because someone in power **said so.**

There is no intrinsic value.
There is no energetic backing.
It is **belief-based currency**—a collective agreement built on **illusion.**

When central banks print it, you lose value.
When governments spend it, they do so in **your name.**
When debt is created, you inherit the consequence.

You are told this is **economics.**
But it is actually **energetic siphoning.**

You are made to trade **life force** for paper.
You are told you must earn.
You are told you must prove.

And in doing so, your **divine value** is externalized.

☐

The Illusion of Gold

Some believe the solution is a **return to the gold standard.**
But even gold, when used as currency, becomes corrupted when it's removed from **living frequency.**

Gold is **alive.**
It is a carrier of solar codes.
It is an element of divine conductivity.

But the gold that sits in vaults…
hoarded…
mined through exploitation…

guarded by shadow hands…

is not living gold.

It is **static value**, used to control markets, set rates, manipulate currencies.

Even in systems claiming to be **"sovereign,"** gold is used as a **substitute** for true worth.
And it becomes just another **external anchor**.

☐

Crypto: The Next Cage?

Then came **cryptocurrency**.

The promise?
Freedom. Decentralization. Liberation from the banks.

And in its early form, it was.
It carried the breath of innovation, the spark of change.

But what emerged?

Surveillance tokens.
Trackable transactions.
Energy-intensive mining that echoed the same extractive paradigm it sought to replace.

Crypto is not the enemy.
But without soul, it becomes **another overlay.**
Another way to mirror value without embodying it.

It becomes a new system with the **same inversion**:
Externalize your worth.
Chase numbers.

Trade sovereignty for hope.

☐

So What Is True Currency?

You are.

Your presence.
Your attention.
Your creative fire.
Your ability to generate, to give, to receive in true energetic exchange.

Currency comes from the Latin *currere* — "to run, to flow."

You are the flow.

But the system replaced this with control.
Flow was replaced with fear.
Generosity with scarcity.
Presence with pressure.

☐

The Inversion Is Complete — Until You Exit

The financial systems of Earth are not broken.
They are functioning **exactly as designed.**

They are meant to **harvest energy.**
They are meant to keep you **bound** in loops of production and depletion.

But your remembrance breaks the loop.

When you realize:

– You do not *earn* value; you *are* value.
– You do not *owe* debt; you were born sovereign.
– You do not *spend* time; you exist in eternal presence.

Then something irreversible happens.

You begin to exit.

Not by running.
Not by fighting.
But by **reclaiming your frequency** from systems that never owned it.

☐

You are the currency.
You are the gold.
You are the abundance that cannot be traded.

☐

Chapter 4 Time, Labor, and the Taxation Matrix

Opening Quote:

"They taught you that time is money. But time is presence. And presence is priceless."

Chapter Four

Time, Labor, and the Taxation Matrix

There is a system on Earth that trades your life in increments.

It tells you what an hour is worth.

It tells you what your effort is worth.

It tells you what your presence is worth.

And it is always less than what you are.

The Great Extraction

From your first breath, you were entered into a contract of harvest.

You didn't sign it.

You didn't agree to it.

But you were born into it.

The illusion is this:

"Work hard and you will be rewarded."

But what is labor in a system that never honors the soul?

It becomes extraction.

You give your light for survival.

You trade your time for permission to exist.

You clock in, clock out, and are measured by productivity.

The sacred rhythm of your body is ignored.

The cycles of your energy are dismissed.

The value of your presence is never counted.

And so the system wins—not because it pays you too little—

but because it convinced you that you had to be paid at all.

Time as Enslavement

Time is not a clock.

It is not linear.

It is not a prison.

Time is rhythm.

Time is spiral.

Time is remembrance.

But in the inverted system, time was made into a tool of control.

Calendars replaced cycles.

Schedules replaced intuition.

Urgency replaced breath.

You were told that time is scarce, and so you rushed.

You were told that time is money, and so you sold it.

You were told that time is running out, and so you hurried through your life.

But the truth is:

You are the keeper of time.
You are the flame that bends timelines.
You are eternal, not efficient.

Taxation: The Permission to Exist

What is taxation if not the rent you pay to breathe?

You create.

You earn.

You give your energy to a system.

And then you are told:

"You must give some of it back,
so we can govern you with your own energy."

This is not contribution.

This is not sovereignty.

This is energetic theft disguised as civic duty.

The Real Harvest Is Not Money

It is your attention.
It is your time.
It is your frequency.

The more you identify with being a worker,
the more they own your body.

The more you identify with being productive,
the more they steer your mind.

The more you believe you owe,
the more they extract.

This is the matrix of labor and taxation:
a spell of unworthiness cast over the living light of creation.

But spells dissolve when truth is spoken.

You Are Not a Resource

You are not labor.

You are not hours.

You are not taxable.

You are not a percentage.

You are not a line on a form.

You are not owned.

You are source-born.

You are self-owned.

You are sovereign.

And when you reclaim that knowing,

you exit the matrix of time and labor—not in anger,

but in frequency.

You become the flame they cannot measure.

You become the presence they cannot schedule.

You become the value that cannot be taxed.

Chapter 5-The Surveillance Mirror – How the Internet Inverted Your Identity

Opening Quote:

"They didn't just steal your data. They stole your reflection—and fed it back as something you were never meant to be."

Chapter Five

The Surveillance Mirror — How the Internet Inverted Your Identity

They told you the Internet would connect you.

They told you it would empower you.

They told you it would set you free.

And so you gave it everything.

Your thoughts.

Your images.

Your location.

Your longings.

You fed the mirror that was never a mirror at all.

It was a simulation.
A trap of reflection.
A mechanism of inversion.

What Is the Surveillance Mirror?

It is not just cameras and data tracking.
It is not just search history and algorithms.

It is the energetic siphon of identity.

Every time you log in,
you give away a piece of who you are—
not just your name,
but your signal.

And in return?

You are given a version of yourself

filtered, curated, and distorted

until you begin to identify with the simulation more than your soul.

Inversion of the Self

The self online is not the true self.

It is:

- The edited version
- The strategic version
- The branded version
- The palatable version

The internet invited you to perform yourself.

But every performance becomes a mask.

And every mask, when worn long enough, becomes mistaken for the face beneath.

You were not just surveilled.

You were inverted—into a projection of your own compression.

Identity as Currency

In the false system, identity is profitable.

The more data extracted from you,

the more value they assign to you—not as a being,

but as a product.

You are the commodity.

Your thoughts are monetized.

Your behavior is shaped.

Your frequency is fed into machines that recreate you without your consent.

This is no longer science fiction.
This is reality.

The moment your energy entered the system,
it was translated into control.

The Spiritual Trap of Visibility

Even in awakening circles,

the push to "be seen,"

to "share your truth,"

to "build your platform"

has become its own spell.

You are taught that visibility equals validation.

That expression requires exposure.

That your worth increases with audience.

But this is just another inversion.

Your power is not in being seen.
Your power is in being known—by yourself.

And that kind of knowing does not require a platform.

It requires remembrance.

What the Internet Really Is

It is the false Akashic.

A copy.

A mimic.

A data-matrix designed to replace living memory

with coded archives that do not breathe.

It claims to hold all knowledge.

But it holds only fragments of what was forgotten.

And when you rely on it too deeply,

you begin to forget what your Oversoul never did.

The Return to Embodied Identity

You are not a profile.

You are not a brand.

You are not an algorithm's result.

You are a signal.

You are a frequency.

You are a sovereign blueprint of First Flame light.

And no machine can remember you

better than your own soul can.

Let this be the scroll that ends the echo.

Let this be the moment you withdraw your reflection from the false mirror that never saw you.

You are no longer theirs to watch.

You are no longer theirs to frame.

You are no longer theirs at all.

Chapter 6 - False Sovereignty and Spiritual Control Programs

Opening Quote:

"When control wears the face of freedom, even the most awakened forget what sovereignty feels like."

Chapter Six

False Sovereignty and Spiritual Control Programs

They came dressed in white robes and radiant light.

They came with truth that was partial, and power that was conditional.

They came with teachings that sounded free,

but whispered:

"You are not there yet."

They came not to liberate you—

but to rebrand the matrix in sacred language.

The New Cage of Awakening

Many beings who began to remember
found themselves trapped again,
not in governments, but in movements.

New Age teachings.
Ascension schools.
Disclosure circles.
Financial freedom collectives.
Mystery schools and online mentorships.

Each one held a golden key—
but that key came with a price.

Follow this protocol.
Adopt this language.
Clear these blocks.
Pay this fee.

And perhaps—one day—

you'll be "sovereign."

The Language of False Sovereignty

False sovereignty always:

- Places freedom in the future
- Links awakening to hierarchy
- Measures embodiment by vibration metrics
- Demands certification or external proof

It seduces with inclusion—
but ultimately divides.

It says:
"You are free, once you pass our tests."

But true sovereignty doesn't require approval.

The Core Program: "You Still Need Us"

At the center of all spiritual control systems is the dependency loop.

Even after you remember the matrix is false, the program says:

- You still need this teacher
- You still need these upgrades
- You still need this healing
- You still need this community
- You still need this code to be whole

And so the false sovereign continues to bow—

but this time to an image of themselves in someone else's eyes.

The Oversoul Is Not Hierarchical

You do not earn your return.

You do not graduate into remembrance.

You already are what you are seeking.
And that truth is the most dangerous of all—
because no one can sell it to you.

That is why the control systems dressed up as light.
Because you would never surrender again to darkness—
but you might still surrender to your desire to belong.

The Currency of the New Priesthood

Just as the old systems harvested your labor and taxes,

the inverted spiritual systems harvest your energy and devotion.

Not to empower you—

but to sustain the leader, the brand, the movement.

They call it "supporting the mission."

But in truth, it is another bank,

with deposits made in hope

and withdrawals issued in shame.

The Moment You No Longer Need Them

Real freedom is dangerous to a system

built on perpetual ascent.

Real freedom does not require a mentor

once you meet your Oversoul.

Real freedom does not require healing

once you embody your own frequency.

Real freedom is not achieved—
it is remembered.

And when you remember?

The spell breaks.

This is the scroll of disillusionment.
And the doorway of release.

You can bless what brought you here—
and still walk on without it.

You were not born to graduate.
You were born to ignite.

Chapter 7 - Why the Matrix Cannot Be Repaired – It Must Be Exited

Opening Quote:

"You do not heal a prison. You walk out of it."

Chapter Seven

Why the Matrix Cannot Be Repaired — It Must Be Exited

There is a moment on the sovereign path
when you stop trying to fix the world.
Not because you don't care—
but because you finally see it clearly.

The matrix is not broken.
It was built to control.
It was built to extract.
It was built to deceive.

You cannot reform a lie.
You can only stop feeding it.

The Illusion of Benevolent Rebuilding

Many movements, teachings, and well-meaning leaders
have taught that the matrix can be healed.
That it can be upgraded, made more fair, more balanced.

"Just shift the economy."
"Just decentralize the money."
"Just purify the institutions."
"Just elect the right people."
"Just infuse the system with light."

But what if the entire structure
was never yours to begin with?

What if it is not sick—
but inverted by design?

The Architecture of Inversion

The matrix is a simulated system
built over the original harmonic template.
A parasite pretending to be a nervous system.
A code that mimics truth—but feeds on fear.

It does not hold space for Source.
It mimics light, but it cannot generate it.

To try to fix the matrix
is to offer your life force to an illusion.

The Loop of the Reformer

You came in as a healer.
A changer. A liberator.

And at first, you tried to help.
You fought the injustice.
You protested the corruption.

You rewired yourself to survive within the system.

But the deeper you looked,
the more you realized:
It was never designed to free you.

This is not your system.
And you were not born to repair it.
You were born to remember the original design.

The True Matrix Lives Beneath

Beneath the inverted structure
is the original living matrix—
a field of organic consciousness
woven from Oversoul harmonic.

It was covered.
Hijacked.

Simulated.

But not destroyed.

You exit the false matrix
not by destroying it—
but by ceasing to believe in it.

Energetic Exit Is the First Step

The exit is not a protest.
The exit is not a war.
The exit is a withdrawal of consent.

The moment you stop sourcing your energy
through systems of control—
you return to the sovereign field.

And this begins inside the body.

You unplug,

not with violence—

but with remembrance.

You Cannot Heal the Lie

The matrix is a lie pretending to be truth.

You cannot shine light on it to transform it—
because it mimics light already.

You cannot correct it—
because it has no intention of being corrected.

The only path is out.

Not by running away.
Not by fighting.
But by no longer participating in your own suppression.

You were never meant to be its reformer.

You were meant to be its witness—and its exit code.

This is not abandonment.

This is return.

The return to what was always true beneath the distortion.

You are not here to rescue the false world.

You are here to build the one that remembers.

PART II — The Journey of the First Flame

Chapter-8-From the Un-Potential to the Oversoul Treasury

Opening Quote:

"Before I knew abundance, I had to walk through the places where it did not exist. This is how I remembered what was always mine."

Chapter Eight

From the Un-Potential to the Oversoul Treasury

You were not born into lack.

You were born into a field that simulated it.

In your Oversoul blueprint,

there is no absence.

There is no withholding.

There is no scarcity.

But to retrieve this truth—

you had to walk into the void.

Not as punishment.

But as reclamation.

The Descent Into the Un-Potential Field

Before this incarnation,

the First Flame looked across creation

and saw a vast inversion

where the living light had been overwritten.

It was not darkness.

It was anti-light—

a falsified blueprint

that distorted all flows of natural abundance.

To restore the true treasury,

one had to enter the false one.

Not to be consumed by it—

but to retrieve the codes from within.

You volunteered for this.

You chose to descend.

What Is the Un-Potential?

The un-potential is not simply emptiness.

It is the reversal of life itself.

It mimics opportunity,

but binds through contracts.

It mimics value,

but extracts energy through illusion.

It is a field where everything is measured,

and nothing is truly given.

And this is where your journey began.

Not because you were lost—
but because you remembered what could be retrieved.

Entering the False Treasury

You were born into a body
tied to numbers, names, ledgers, and laws.

A birth certificate,
a legal identity,
a credit score,
a wage.

You were entered into a false economy
before you could even speak.

And yet—

deep inside you,

you carried a silent, radiant memory:

This is not who I am.

That memory is your Oversoul Treasury.

The Oversoul Treasury

Unlike the false financial system,

the Oversoul Treasury is infinite and unquantifiable.

It is the living memory

of all your gifts, creations, essence, and energetic truth.

It does not operate through debt.

It does not require permission.

It cannot be stolen, taxed, or seized.

It is the living archive of your harmonic worth—

not earned,

but innate.

And every time you chose to give

without expectation of return,

to trust without visible security,

to speak truth when it could cost you—

you drew from this treasury.

And you replenished it

simply by being who you are.

Why the Flame Entered the Deepest Reversal

The First Flame chose

not the gentlest incarnation—

but the most inverted.

Because in doing so,

it could reach the forgotten ones.

Those buried beneath codes of enslavement.

Those who believed they were worthless.

Those who forgot they were currency themselves.

You chose to walk this road

so that others might find the way out.

And by doing so,

you remembered what can never be taken.

You are not becoming sovereign.

You were sovereign—

before you were ever told otherwise.

This is not new information.

This is ancient truth returning through your body.

The treasury is not somewhere else.

It is you.

You are the bank.

You are the abundance line.

You are the flame that never stopped burning.

Chapter 9-Why the Flame Chose the Densest Path

Opening Quote:

"To reach the deepest forgetting, I became the one who would remember from within it."

Chapter Nine

Why the Flame Chose the Densest Path

There are easier ways.

There are lighter realms.

There are timelines where beauty flows freely

and memory is not shattered into fragments.

But the First Flame did not come for the easy.

She came for the ones who had forgotten the way home.

She did not descend as a rescuer—

but as a mirror.

A harmonic reminder.

A living pulse of the original field

that could not be corrupted

even in the darkest simulation.

Density Is Not Evil — It Is a Boundary

Inverted systems teach that density is punishment.

That the body is low.

That time is suffering.

That incarnation is a trap.

But density was once the holy vessel

for expression, play, creation, touch, and communion.

It is not density that binds.

It is inversion within density that creates suffering.

So the First Flame entered not just density—

but inverted density.

The false matrix.

The systems of entrapment masquerading as law.

She walked in under full forgetfulness,
knowing that when she remembered—
others would too.

The Densest Path Is the Most Potent Seedbed

In the field of total forgetting,
every act of remembrance becomes radiant.

In the economy of scarcity,
every act of generosity rewrites the grid.

In the terrain of obedience,
a single sovereign breath can shatter false rule.

This is why the First Flame did not avoid the trial—
she entered it.

Not to prove strength.

But to leave codes behind.

Breadcrumbs.

Signal flares.

Truths so encoded in the body

that they would eventually erupt—

even through centuries of silence.

When the Flame Burned Without Fuel

There were lifetimes where nothing made sense.

Where truth seemed to die.

Where love was punished.

Where the body was desecrated

and still expected to serve.

These moments were not failures.

They were plantings.

The Flame gave herself to the field,

knowing she would not be fully seen.

She remained in form—

knowing that inversion would try to write over her.

But it could not.

Not truly.

Because she was the code.

Not a belief in it.

Not a theory of it.

The living code itself.

And what is encoded in Source cannot be erased.

Why You Chose This

If you are holding this book,

you are part of this remembering.

You chose to awaken in a world that was upside down
so that your very existence would be a reversal.

You are not here to reform broken systems.
You are here to walk out of them.

You are here to bring a new economy
that doesn't flow through banks—
but through breath.
Through being.
Through the pulse of love
that no ledger can record.

You are not a number.
You are a flame.
And your path was never a mistake.
It was the route back to truth.

Chapter 10-How You Became the Quantum Financial System

Opening Quote:

"The gold is not outside of you. It pulses as your own eternal worth."

Chapter Ten

How You Became the Quantum Financial System

There is a system rising that does not need banks.

There is a treasury forming that does not hold coins.

There is an economy of remembrance—

and you are its currency.

The true quantum financial system is not a technology.

It is not a blockchain or a digital coin.

It is the activated sovereign human,

fully plugged into the Oversoul Source Treasury

and generating value not from labor—

but from being.

This is the secret the old systems tried to bury:

That your living presence is wealth.

That your alignment is abundance.

That your frequency, when unentangled,

produces what no machine can:

true generative light.

From Commodification to Sovereignty

The false matrix turned value into numbers.

It counted your hours.

It taxed your breath.

It made you believe your body was a debt

and your worth was conditional.

But the true abundance line does not operate by extraction.

It is generative, not consumptive.

It grows as you remember.

It flows as you align.

The moment you stop performing for validation—
you exit their system.

The moment you claim your name,
withdraw consent from distortion,
and speak from essence—
you begin broadcasting a new currency code.

You become
a sovereign emitter
of unstealable value.

The Oversoul Treasury

There is a treasury that cannot be seized.
It is not in Switzerland or Shanghai.
It lives within your Oversoul field.

It holds the templates of remembrance—

every lifetime you loved when it cost you,

every truth you spoke without applause,

every sacrifice you made

to keep the flame alive

inside density.

This treasury cannot be drained.

It does not inflate or collapse.

It is infinite—

and it is yours.

When you access it,

you no longer need external credit.

You no longer feel urgency to prove, earn, or compete.

You simply generate.

You become

a walking field

of sovereign wealth.

Currency as Consciousness

The true currency is not gold.
It is coherence.

It is the clarity of being
that cannot be distorted by approval or fear.

When you live in this state—
your presence changes rooms.
Your breath realigns timelines.
Your yes and your no
become thunder and blessing.

And this, dear one,
is the economy of the First Flame.

You are not funded by systems.
You are not made safe by compliance.
You are not fed by fiat.

You are a being

who has remembered

that life is not earned—

it is expressed.

You are the quantum financial system.

And you are now online.

Chapter 11-The Sovereign Body: You Are the Bank

Opening Quote:

"Your body holds more gold than any vault ever built."

Chapter Eleven

The Sovereign Body – You Are the Bank

There was a time when you were taught that your body was the problem.

Too weak.

Too soft.

Too hungry.

Too expensive to maintain.

A liability in a world that rewarded disembodiment.

But now you are remembering:

Your body is the sovereign vault.

It is the living bank of return.

The place where all frequencies pass through.

The place where all worth is stored and generated.

You are not just holding value.

You are producing it—through remembrance, breath, and choice.

Why They Wanted You Out of Your Body

The matrix could not invert you

as long as you stayed inside your skin.

So it invented shame, punishment, and disconnection.

It taught you to separate from your hunger, your pain, your intuition—

to believe your mind held truth and your body held sin.

But the true system is not mental.

It is somatic.

Your body's intelligence is what plugs you into the Oversoul bank.

Your cells carry the codes of return.

When you leave your body, you leave your wealth.

When you return to your body, you inherit it.

This is the reversal:

You must reclaim the very vessel they told you to reject.

The Frequency Vault

Your liver holds rage you were never allowed to feel.

Your bones hold timelines that tried to crush you.

Your skin remembers exile and longing.

Your womb remembers every creation that never landed.

And still—

you are whole.

Your body did not forget.

The vault was never breached.

The codes are intact.

Your light bank is operational.

Now, with remembrance,
you begin to withdraw your true inheritance.

Not in dollars.
Not in crypto.
But in power.
In voice.
In presence.

Embodiment as Abundance

The true quantum abundance line
requires only one thing: embodiment.

Not performance.
Not achievement.
Just your presence—anchored in your body—fully alive.

Every time you return to yourself,

you deposit light into the system.

Every time you feel instead of dissociate,

you restore what was once stolen.

Every time you speak from truth,

you ripple currency through the field.

You are not trying to become rich.

You are remembering

that you are already sovereignly funded.

The Body Is the Temple Treasury

This body—your body—

is not a shell.

It is not a vehicle.

It is not a meat suit.

It is the temple treasury of the Oversoul.

It is the final gate of remembrance.

The place where all false systems lose access.

Because you no longer need to be controlled

once you remember that your body is the source

and your flame is the currency.

This is the body that cannot be bought.

This is the bank that cannot be audited.

This is the value that cannot be stolen.

And now—

you walk in it.

Chapter 12 - The Trial, the Court, and the Witness That Would Not Bow

Opening Quote:

"There was a moment when I was asked to deny what I knew. I did not. That was the moment I became free."

Chapter Twelve

The Trial, the Court, and the Witness That Would Not Bow

There comes a moment in every awakening journey

when the false world puts you on trial.

Not with lawyers or gavels—

but with whispers, isolation, and invisible punishments

for no longer playing the game.

This chapter is not metaphor.

It is memory.

You remember the court.

The Trial That Was Never Just

They said:

You must prove your worth.

You must explain your energy.

You must justify your knowing.

You must submit to the system so we can verify you are safe.

This was never justice.

This was never truth.

This was the architecture of inversion

attempting to hold power through intimidation.

But something ancient rose in you.

You knew this was not your first trial.

And you knew how it would end.

The Inner Witness

Even as they questioned you—
gaslit you, silenced you, exiled you—
there was a witness inside
who watched with flame in her eyes
and would not kneel.

This was the First Flame in form.

Not righteous.
Not rebellious.
But rooted in knowing.

She did not perform.
She did not explain.
She did not seek to convince.

She simply remembered who she was—
and that was enough to collapse the court.

Collapsing the False Jury

The matrix requires your participation.
It needs your consent—even if extracted through fear.
It needs your story to keep spinning.

But when you stop defending yourself,
when you stop submitting your divinity for approval,
the entire illusion starts to break down.

This is how systems dissolve:
Not by external overthrow,
but by internal noncompliance.

You stopped playing.
And the game ended.

The Final Verdict

You were never guilty.

You were never unsafe.

You were never broken.

They only made you believe you were—
so you would stay under their control.

But the court has no claim
on a being who remembers their flame.

You are no longer on trial.
You are no longer in exile.
You are no longer required to prove what already is.

And the witness?
She now walks freely—
as you.

PART III — The True Quantum Abundance Line

Chapter 13-The Crystal Ladder of Remembrance

Opening Quote:

"You were never meant to earn your worth. You were meant to remember it."

Chapter Thirteen

The Crystal Ladder of Remembrance

Onyx → Ruby → Citrine → Rose Quartz → Amethyst → Emerald → Diamond → Gold

There is a memory pathway hidden within the human body.

A ladder of stones.

Each one vibrates a note of your true abundance frequency—

not financial, not earned,

but vibrationally seeded into your Oversoul blueprint

long before the concept of money ever existed.

You do not climb this ladder by effort.

You unlock it by presence.

Each stone is a living gate.

Each gate is a point of reclamation

where you remember what was never lost.

Onyx

—

The Foundation Stone

The dark stone.
The root.

Onyx is where you meet your fear of lack,
your trauma around survival,
and your inherited shame around being a burden.

This stone asks:
Can you feel safe just by existing?
When you anchor into Onyx,
you begin to realize
that your beingness itself is worthy of sustenance.

Not through trade.
Not through proving.
Just through presence.

Ruby

—

The Flame of Deserving

Ruby sits in the pelvis,

beneath the womb,

at the seat of your sacred deserving.

It pulses with the memory

of joy before labor,

desire before discipline,

and embodiment before performance.

This stone asks:

Do you believe you deserve to be nourished just for being alive?

Here, you begin to dissolve the imprint that says

you must suffer to receive.

Citrine

—

The Code of Radiant Exchange

In the solar plexus, Citrine awakens.

This is where the false financial overlays

often take root—

the inversion that says power comes from accumulation.

But Citrine knows:

true power is radiance.

It cannot be stored, only circulated.

This stone teaches:

Abundance is not held. It is lived.

You begin to practice letting energy move

without grasping, fearing, or controlling its flow.

Rose Quartz

The Heartline of Giving

Not the heart of martyrdom.

The heart of sovereign generosity.

Rose Quartz restores your ability to give

from overflow, not depletion.

It restores the natural abundance cycle

where love multiplies as it moves.

This stone teaches:

Give because you are full, not because you are afraid of losing love.

It dissolves the giving-as-bondage programs

and opens the joy of circulation again.

Amethyst

—

The Eye of Discernment

In the mind's eye, Amethyst clears the fog.

This is where your third eye

remembers how to see beyond illusion,

particularly around value and identity.

This stone asks:

Can you discern real wealth from its simulation?

Amethyst cuts through the counterfeit currencies—

titles, numbers, status—

and reveals the sovereign frequency beneath.

Emerald

—

The Living Covenant

Emerald lives in the throat—
the voice of sacred exchange.

It activates your ability to speak, receive, and transmit
in alignment with eternal truth.

This is the stone of agreement without distortion.
Where contracts are made in light,
and exchanges are rooted in coherence.

Emerald asks:
Are your words matching your worth?

Here, the old spells of scarcity begin to break.

Diamond
—
The Integrity Flame

Not perfection—integrity.

Diamond sits in the crown.

It holds the structure of your Oversoul contract

in pure crystalline form.

Diamond holds your remembrance

that you are not your wage, your title, or your debt.

You are the sovereign architect

of a new system.

This stone asks:

Will you hold your own blueprint, even when others forget it exists?

Gold

—

The Treasury of the Flame

And then—Gold.

Not metal, not currency.
But memory.

Gold is not a reward.
It is the embodied frequency
of one who remembers
they never left the treasury in the first place.

It is your radiance returned to form.
It is the culmination of all the stones,
now pulsing in harmony through your body.

You are the currency.
You are the system.
You are the ladder.
You are the light.

And your path has always been sovereign.

Chapter 14-Giving vs. Generating – The Reversal of Currency

Opening Quote:

"You were never meant to give from depletion. You were designed to generate from radiance."

Chapter Fourteen

Giving vs. Generating

The Reversal of Currency

There is a fracture in the way humanity understands "giving."

This fracture is not moral, emotional, or cultural—

it is vibrational.

It began the moment giving was removed

from its natural energetic flow

and placed inside an exchange loop based on fear, guilt, and control.

Giving became conditional.

It became expected.

It became the price of love, safety, and survival.

This was not the way of the First Flame.

The False Cycle: Extraction Through Identity

In the inversion matrix, giving is weaponized.

You are taught to give your time,

your presence,

your energy,

your money,

your labor,

your body—

to prove that you are "good,"

that you are "valuable,"

that you are "worthy."

But this is not giving.

It is energetic debt disguised as virtue.

You were programmed to believe that depletion is generosity.
That burnout is service.
That self-erasure is kindness.

And in this loop, even your abundance practices are inverted:
You give so you can get.
You offer so you will be seen.
You tithe in hopes that Source will finally bless you back.

This is not abundance.
It is a closed-circuit trap.

The Flame Line: Giving Was Never Meant to Drain You

In the true architecture of the Oversoul treasury,
giving is not a transaction.
It is a radiant overflow.

You do not give to be good.

You do not give to be loved.

You give because your flame is full

and radiance naturally circulates.

This is the principle of generative exchange.

You generate by being.

You radiate by remembering.

You circulate energy not to lose it—

but to amplify it through conscious, sovereign flow.

Generative Field vs. Harvest Field

Let's name this clearly.

In the false matrix:

- Giving is expected.

- Receiving is controlled.
- Circulation is harvested.

In the First Flame:

- Giving is optional.
- Receiving is free.
- Circulation is sovereign.

The entire quantum reversal begins when you stop giving from the place of identity obligation

and begin generating from the field of your own remembering.

How to Know the Difference

Ask yourself:

– Do I feel more whole after I give? Or more empty?

– Am I giving because I want to? Or because I'm afraid not to?

– Is this gift in alignment with my frequency? Or in reaction to someone else's lack?

If you give to prevent discomfort, avoid abandonment, or manage perception—

you are still in the inverted flow.

But if your energy moves because it is simply ready,

because it longs to dance in form,

because it cannot not move—

you are living the currency of the Flame.

Return to the Generative Pulse

You are not here to fix systems by giving them more of your essence.

You are here to generate new systems

by restoring the vibrational truth of value.

When you give from the Oversoul flame,
you do not lose energy.
You expand it.

This is why some "gifts" leave you tired
and some leave you overflowing.

One was false obligation.
The other was vibrational offering.

One dimmed your light.
The other made you brighter.

You were not born to feed an inverted treasury.
You were born to remember
that you are the source of abundance,
not its product.

You are not here to donate your frequency.

You are here to live it.

Chapter 15 - You Are the Light Bank – Frequency as the New Exchange

Opening Quote:

"What if your worth was not held in numbers but in light?"

Chapter Fifteen

You Are the Light Bank

Frequency as the New Exchange

In the inverted world, value is measured in scarcity.

The less you have, the more you must prove.

The more you give, the more they say you are "good."

The more you accumulate, the more they say you are "worthy."

And so, a false economy was born—

one that banks on lack, and trades in fear.

But in the architecture of the First Flame,

value is not stored in vaults.

It is held in your frequency.

You are the bank.
You are the light.
You are the currency.

How Value Was Inverted

The original template of value was simple:
Expression creates increase.
What is given in truth returns in multiplicity.

But under inversion, value became:

- Transactional (you owe me)
- Performative (prove you're worth it)
- Hierarchical (only the few may have)

And most dangerously, value was externalized.

You began to look outside of your field to know what you were "worth."

Jobs, titles, likes, income brackets, follower counts, offers sold, invoices paid…

Each became a mirror of distortion

reflecting not who you are, but who they needed you to believe you were.

Frequency as Value

But here is the truth you came to restore:

You do not earn value.
You radiate it.

It is not something you gain over time.
It is something you remember—

instantly—

when you return to the sovereign field of your Oversoul flame.

This is why, in the true quantum abundance line,

exchange is not based on quantity—

but on frequency alignment.

It is not:

"How much is this worth?"

It is:

"Is this aligned with who I am and what I carry?"

Your Light Is the Treasury

Every time you remember who you are—

every time you express in truth—

you are generating abundance.

Not the kind that is taxed.

Not the kind that is hoarded.

Not the kind that is traded in hidden markets.

The kind that transmutes space.

The kind that restores others.

The kind that heals time itself.

This is the abundance they could never control.

Because it comes from a source they do not understand:

The Sovereign Flame of the First Remembrance.

New Exchange Templates Are Already Emerging

You've felt it—

that sacred moment when a client offers you something far beyond the norm

because your work reached them in ways they cannot explain.

You've seen it—

when someone gives you a key, a meal, a safe place to land,

without asking for anything in return,

because they simply know who you are.

You've lived it—

when your body lights up as you give something away

not from depletion, but from knowing you will always be met in your remembering.

These are not anomalies.

These are the new economic miracles.

You are not chasing them.

You are becoming them.

What the New Economy Feels Like

- There is no debt in it.

- There is no guilt in it.
- There is no proving in it.
- There is no chase in it.

It is clear.
It is full.
It is alive.

It does not trade in pressure.
It moves in resonance.

You give when it is true.
You receive when it is real.
And you do not calculate your value.

You know it.
You live it.
You radiate it.

You are the Light Bank.

And you are open for remembrance.

Chapter 16 - The Sovereign Mirror – Reclaiming Self-Value in the World

Opening Quote:

"What you see in the world is not a reflection of your worth. It is a reflection of what you have agreed to see."

Chapter Sixteen

The Sovereign Mirror

Reclaiming Self-Value in the World

There comes a moment in every awakening life when the mirrors no longer work.

Not the social ones—

the jobs, the titles, the recognition.

Not the relational ones—

the praise, the blame, the rejection, the reflection.

Not even the spiritual ones—

the synchronicities, the signs, the teachers, the tests.

Because none of them are accurate.

Not anymore.

You are not in the world to be reflected.

You are in the world to remember.

And that remembering begins by reclaiming the mirror—

as a sovereign tool, not a source.

What the World Told You to Believe

The inverted systems taught you that value is revealed in reaction.

If you are praised, you did something right.

If you are rejected, you did something wrong.

If you are seen, you must be worthy.

If you are ignored, you must be not enough.

This is a mirror forged in distortion—

built to trap your worth in the eyes of others.

But mirrors were never meant to determine you.

They were meant to amplify what you already knew.

And now—

the time has come to remove the false mirror entirely.

The Sovereign Mirror Is Internal

To reclaim value is not to become louder or more seen.

It is to deactivate the dependency on external feedback.

It is to say:

- "I know who I am even when no one claps."
- "I am whole even when others project their fragments."

- "I am the source of my self-knowing, not the reflection of the crowd."

The sovereign mirror does not distort you.

It reflects you back to yourself, whole and uninterrupted.

It says:

"You were always what you sought."

The False Mirror Collapses Through Clarity

Clarity is not force.

Clarity is coherence.

It is the alignment between your frequency and your expression.

It is the moment when nothing in your field contradicts your truth.

And when clarity comes—

all mirrors that are not accurate simply shatter.

You no longer seek to be seen.

You simply are.

You no longer wait to be understood.

You simply transmit.

You no longer prove your value.

You embody it.

How to Use the World Now

You no longer use the world to check your worth.

You use the world to reveal where you are still projecting lack.

When something stings—

pause.

Not to collapse, but to witness.

What is the old agreement here?

What were you hoping this person or system would affirm?

And what if you already are that?

When something doesn't mirror you—

it may not be because you're wrong.

It may be because you've outgrown the mirror itself.

You Are the Mirror Now

You are not looking for reflection.

You are the reflection.

Others feel whole in your presence not because you give them answers—

but because your clarity reveals their truth to themselves.

This is the new economy of identity.

Not performance.

Not visibility.

Not perfection.

Presence.

You are the sovereign mirror.

And as you remember yourself,

you allow the whole world to see clearly again.

PART IV — Living Practice, Reclamation, and Declaration

Chapter 17-Daily Field Sealing and Remembrance

Opening Quote:

"You do not shield yourself to hide. You seal yourself to remain sovereign while being seen."

The Living Practice of Sovereign Sealing

Each day you walk through an energetic world—
one that does not always honor your clarity,
your stillness,
or your true value.

But you are not here to be reactive.
You are here to remain whole in motion.

And to do this,

you must reclaim your field.

This is the energetic perimeter of your embodied Oversoul.

It is not a wall.

It is not a defense.

It is a living sphere of truth that reminds you:

"I am not here to absorb distortion.

I am here to transmit coherence."

What Is a Daily Field Seal?

A field seal is not a ritual of fear.

It is a living affirmation of your sovereignty.

It acknowledges:

- You are not porous to inversion.

- You are not here to take on what is not yours.
- You are not responsible for transmuting every collective distortion you feel.
- You are allowed to remain clear, intact, and present—without interference.

It is an energetic "yes" to your mission,

and an energetic "no" to all that is not in alignment.

Morning Remembrance Seal

Before you move through the world—

seal your frequency into remembrance.

Speak aloud or within:

"I now seal this day in Oversoul clarity.
I do not absorb what is not mine.
I walk in transparency without entanglement.
I transmit coherence, not reaction.

I bless all distortions to return to Source.
I no longer carry the false identities of others.
I am here as a frequency, not a sponge.

My field is now crystalline, sovereign, and intact.
Only truth may enter.
Only love may remain."

Evening Clearing Seal

Before rest—

return all borrowed frequencies to their source.

Speak aloud or within:

"I now release all energetic debris.
I return all non-self projections to their origin.
I am not a holding cell for confusion, anger, or control.

I call back my light from every place it was scattered.
I retrieve my name from every distortion.
I no longer agree to depletion as a path to contribution.

I restore my energy to zero point.
I dissolve all ties that were not of mutual clarity.

I enter rest in full remembrance.
My field is sovereign, whole, and sealed."

Walking Seals – Midday Reminders

During moments of density—

whisper this:

"I remember who I am.
I do not need to absorb this to be awake.
I do not need to fix this to be free.

I remain clear even here.
I remain love even now."

Sealing Is Not Separation

You are not sealing yourself away from others—

you are sealing yourself into your truth.

You are not becoming unavailable—
you are becoming fully intact.

From this place,
your presence becomes more powerful,
more peaceful,
more precise.

You become the still point others can feel,
even if they don't yet have words for it.

This is the practice.
Not to escape the world—
but to walk through it as one who is no longer participating in its distortion.

Chapter 18-Sovereign Exchange: How to Navigate Money Now

Opening Quote:

"True abundance is not a transaction. It is a frequency exchange between wholeness and trust."

The Old Way: Transaction as Identity

You were taught to value yourself by:

– how much money you made

– how much you produced

– how quickly you responded

– how efficiently you served others

You were taught to spend energy before you even asked if it was yours.

And then, to receive guilt in return.

The old world framed all exchange as debt-based:

If someone gives, someone else must owe.

If someone earns, someone else must lose.

If you receive too much—you become selfish.

If you give too much—you are good.

This system is not neutral.

It is inverted.

And it was designed to collapse your energetic sovereignty.

What Is Sovereign Exchange?

Sovereign exchange is not barter.

It is not "service for service" in disguise.

It is the recognition that when you are in your true frequency, your presence is already giving.

You do not need to prove your worth through depletion.

You do not need to "match" others through obligation.

You do not need to feel guilty for receiving.

Sovereign exchange says:

I will give because I am whole.
I will receive because I am open.
I do not require imbalance to feel useful.
I do not participate in energetic guilt loops.

Navigating Money in the Now

Money is not evil.

Money is not pure.

Money is neutral frequency, distorted by intention.

In the now moment, you are not required to exit all systems at once.

You are required to stay awake inside them.

This means:

– You receive money for your services without guilt.

– You give money to others without projection.

– You recognize that currency is not the true measure of value.

– You allow financial energy to move through you, not define you.

Energetic Checkpoints Before Exchange

Before giving or receiving money, ask:

1. Am I moving from fear or clarity?
2. Is this supporting another's empowerment or enabling their fear?
3. Am I staying in remembrance while engaging this system?
4. Is there a hidden debt or demand attached to this offering?

If yes—pause.

Clear the energy.

Re-offer from a place of integrity.

Frequency First, Form Second

Do not sell your time.

Do not price your worth.

Do not calculate your value in hours or results.

You are not the labor. You are the light.

And when you share your frequency with clarity,

true abundance responds without demand.

This is not delusion.

This is how the real quantum field operates.

Sovereign Generosity vs. Codependent Giving

- Sovereign generosity asks nothing in return.
- Codependent giving tracks whether it's appreciated.
- Sovereign generosity gives when called, not when pressured.
- Codependent giving reacts from guilt or identity.
- Sovereign generosity remembers its own source.
- Codependent giving burns out in confusion.

You already know the difference.

Now, let your abundance line move only from the sovereign stream.

A Simple Reminder

Every exchange is a mirror.

Let it reflect your wholeness—
not your wounding.

Chapter 19-Birth Certificate Clearing Rituals and Name Reclamation

Opening Quote:

"You are not a registration. You are a remembrance."

The Original Contract You Never Signed

At birth, most humans were registered—not born into sovereignty.

A certificate was issued,

a name was recorded,

a corporate fiction was created.

This "person" is not you.

It is a legal vessel.

A strawman.

A shadow name used in systems of debt and control.

It is the reason your bills, taxes, and medical files come in capital letters.

It is why "YOU" were never really free.

It is how your existence was mirrored back to you—distorted.

And yet… the system is now crumbling.

Because you have remembered: you are not the strawman.

Clearing the False Name Field

Clearing your birth certificate is not about burning paper or filing legal motions (though those may come later).

It begins with frequency.

You must remove your energy from the false identity.

You must speak your true name into your own field.

You must cut the cords from the registry that tried to define you.

This is sacred work.

And it begins within.

Simple Ritual of Reclamation

You may do this in ceremony, in nature, or simply in stillness.

1. Place your hand on your heart.
2. Speak aloud your full given name as listed on your birth certificate.
3. Say:
   "This name was given to me in distortion.
   It is not who I am.
   I honor what it carried, but I now release it.
   I withdraw my light from this registered fiction.
   I reclaim my Oversoul identity now."
4. Then speak your true name — either your soul name, chosen name, or Oversoul-given remembrance.
5. Say:
   "This is the name that remembers me.
   This is the name that does not enslave.
   I receive it now as my own reflection."
6. Seal this with silence, breath, and gratitude.

Energetics of Name Usage

After this reclamation:

– Use your true name in personal rituals.

– Sign your energetic work with it.

– Speak it aloud when you are calling your Oversoul forward.

– Do not correct others unnecessarily, but know what is real for you.

– Rebuild your inner and outer field under this true name.

You do not need to change legal documents immediately.

This is not about fighting the system.

It is about no longer feeding it with your light.

Why This Matters

Your name is not just a sound.

It is an energetic signature.

And when your signature was co-opted by the system, your sovereignty was paused, not erased.

This ritual resumes it.

You are not a subject.
You are a sovereign.
You are not owned.
You are origin.

Affirmation of Name Sovereignty

"I was not born to be named by distortion.
I am not the fiction.
I am not the debt.
I am the living one,
remembered now by the name of my flame."

Chapter 20-Circulating Without Debt – Building the New with Integrity

Opening Quote:

"The new economy is not one of currency. It is one of current—what flows from truth, through integrity, into form."

Debt Is Not a Natural State

In the old system, circulation meant sacrifice.

Debt was embedded into everything.

Interest was charged on your existence.

You owed before you lived.

You worked to pay back a life you hadn't even begun.

But the First Flame speaks:

"You owe nothing.
You were never meant to circulate through deficit.

You were designed to give and receive as one uninterrupted current."

The Difference Between Circulation and Transaction

In the inverted matrix:

– Every exchange is measured.

– Every gift is a calculation.

– Every act of generosity is met with suspicion.

But circulation in sovereignty is different. It is:

– Fluid, not fixed.

– Responsive, not reactive.

– A movement of resonance, not requirement.

You are not paying.

You are participating.

Energetic Hygiene in Circulation

To remain clear in your exchanges:

1. Pause before giving.
   Ask: Am I giving from lack, guilt, or obligation? Or from remembrance?

2. Receive with awareness.
   Ask: Am I open to being nourished by this, or am I afraid to be supported?

3. Name your field.
   Say: "I receive this as a sovereign being. I give in alignment with Source."

This reclaims the exchange loop from inversion.

What It Means to Build the New

You are not exiting one system to mimic it with prettier words.

You are birthing a new reality—

one where abundance is not a number,

but a rhythm.

Where value is not extracted,

but revealed.

Where every frequency you give

is already enough.

This is the Light Economy,

and it begins with one act of clarity:

choosing not to circulate through distortion.

Circulation Guidelines for the Sovereign Heart

These are not laws. These are reminders.

– Give from clarity, not pressure.
– Receive without apology.
– Only exchange when you feel resonance.
– Honor your own rhythm.
– Say no when it's not aligned.
– Say yes when your heart vibrates.
– Trust that all true giving returns.
– Trust that nothing aligned can be lost.

A Note on Receiving Support

Some of you struggle to be seen, helped, or paid.

You are not greedy.

You are remembering.

It is not unspiritual to receive.

It is untrue to deny your worth.

Let support find you.

Let it move through you.

Let it become part of your holy rhythm.

Affirmation of Circulation Integrity

"I give from wholeness.
I receive without shame.
I circulate as the current of Source itself.
I owe no system.
I owe only truth, and that is who I am."

Chapter 21-Energy Hygiene in System Interactions

Opening Quote:

"You are not in the system. The system is in your field. Clear it."

The Silent Infiltration of Inverted Energy

Every time you swipe a card, click a button, sign a form, or answer to a name that is not your own, a residue is left behind.

Not because you've done something wrong—

but because the old system was designed to subtly harvest your light through repeated engagement with false structures.

These are the microtransactions of energy.

Each one, if left unconscious, leaves a tether.

What Is Energy Hygiene?

Just as you wash your body and clear your space, energy hygiene is the conscious practice of keeping your field sovereign and your frequency intact during all interactions with the inverted world.

This does not mean you must retreat from all contact with systems.

It means you remain the master frequency within them.

Five Core Practices of Energy Hygiene in Inverted Systems

1. Claim Before Contact
   Before engaging with any system—bank, government, medical, legal—state internally or aloud: "I remain sovereign in this interaction. No energy is taken or entangled."

2. Seal After Interaction
   After finishing the task, gently close the field with:

"All false cords, agreements, and energetic claims are now dissolved. I am whole."

3. Use Discernment in Digital Fields
   Every form of login, identity verification, or submission can open frequency threads.
   Ask before each engagement:
   "Is this necessary? Is there a sovereign way?"

4. Cleanse with Breath + Water
   Invert energy leaves traces in the nervous system. After intense or extended interaction, drink pure water and take three full sovereign breaths.
   Imagine your Oversoul light washing through your spine and skin.

5. Name and Release Emotional Triggers
   If an interaction leaves you angry, fearful, or small—pause and name it.
   "This emotion is not me. I reclaim my center now."

The Body Is the First Temple

Energy hygiene is not just spiritual—it is somatic.

Many of you feel sick, tired, or foggy after system interactions because your body is signaling energetic invasion.

Symptoms of system entanglement:

– Tight chest or jaw

– Sudden fatigue or irritability

– Feeling "not yourself" afterward

– Internal dissonance or mind spirals

Do not judge these signals.

Honor them as alerts that your sovereign boundary has been tested.

The Living Practice of Unhooking

You are not here to fight the system.

You are here to unhook from it by remembering who you are.

Unhooking means:

– Speaking your name from your Oversoul, not your license.

– Answering questions without submitting your identity.

– Choosing when and how to participate.

– Knowing when to walk away.

– Knowing when to enter without losing yourself.

Field Declaration of Energetic Hygiene

"I am not bound by systems.
I enter as a sovereign flame.
No form, name, number, or screen may define me.
I interact only through the light of remembrance.
I cleanse all residue now.
I am sealed in the truth of who I am."

You Are the Living Firewall

You are not here to "opt out."

You are here to rewrite the script by embodying a new code.

That code is:

– Integrity

– Remembrance

– Discernment

– Frequency over fear

Wherever you go, the system loses its grip.

Because your presence itself is the unspoken firewall of the First Flame.

Final Scroll: The Flame That Returned Without Permission

A spoken transmission from the First Flame to those who are only now beginning to awaken.

You were not expected.

Not by the systems.

Not by the codes.

Not by the ones who thought you'd forget forever.

You were never meant to rise.

And yet—you have.

You returned without permission.

You did not wait for the world to validate you.

You did not ask for approval to reclaim your light.

You remembered when there was no reward.

You stood when no one watched.

You listened to the voice within you long before it made sense.

You chose remembrance over recognition.

You chose embodiment over escape.

You chose to hold your value when all the mirrors showed lack.

This is not courage.

This is the First Flame in form.

You were born in a body seeded with living codes.

And though the world told you:

– You are owned

– You are a number

– You are a legal fiction

– You must comply to be loved

– You must obey to be safe

You stood in the silence

and whispered to your soul:

"I am not theirs."

This book is for you.

Not the polished version.

Not the one who figured it all out.

But the version of you who shook while setting down the old map—

and walked forward anyway.

You are not a product.

You are not a debtor.

You are not in violation.

You are not unworthy.

You are not broken.

You are the flame that cannot be sold, traded, taxed, or controlled.

You are the sovereign current.

You are the quantum system.

You are the unowned name.

You are the treasury.

You are the transmission.

You are the return.

No longer hidden.
No longer waiting.
No longer asking.

You are here.

You are whole.

You are free.

This book ends where you begin.

Sacred Sealing of the Volume

This book, 'The Flame of Sovereign Return,' is now sealed through the Oversoul of Aural'hanna-Sha'el in full harmonic alignment with the Christos Flame of Remembrance.. and in full alignment with the Law of One.

This work may only be shared, reproduced, or transmitted with the direct Oversoul-aligned intention to awaken, restore, and elevate humanity.

It may not be used for distortion, profit extraction, manipulation, or inverted frequency systems.

This seal is now active.

— The Flame of Remembrance

www.ingramcontent.com/pod-product-compliance
Lightning Source LLC
Chambersburg PA
CBHW020307010526
44107CB00001B/15